SUMMARY OF

A PLAGUE UPON OUR HOUSE

MY FIGHT AT THE TRUMP WHITE HOUSE TO STOP COVID FROM DESTROYING AMERICA

SCOTT W. ATLAS, MD

Cherry Katherine

D1528080

TABLE OF CONTENTS

INTRODUCTION
A Broken Trust

Government officials, public health officials, and scientists remain unaccountable because they do not admit to errors about lockdowns; some even falsify their records and present catastrophic deaths as "successes. "The CDC and public health officials still do not recognize natural immunity in cured COVID patients and do not inform the public about it or incorporate this biological fact into our nation's vaccine policies.

The public needs to know that there is growing evidence that natural immunity after SARS2 infection, as with other infectious diseases, is probably superior to vaccine-related protection.

Public health officials and key government representatives continue to use wildly inaccurate predictions that scare and worry the public, and when they are wrong, they fail to admit this fact.

Our public health recommendations on masks and distancing were not changed after scientific data showed that the previous rules were arbitrary, wrong, and ineffective.

Do we have to prove again that the Earth is round? Serious problems with the data, including the excess of COVIDs causing many hospitalizations and deaths in the United States, have never been explained to the public or acknowledged, although they are documented in the medical literature.

The nation is still waiting for word that a full investigation will be conducted into the origin of the deadly virus, even as it reveals possible corruption among our nation's top science agencies and public health officials.

The handling of this pandemic has tainted many once noble American institutions, including our elite universities, research institutes and journals, and public health agencies.

Even if one believed in the health benefits of these diktats, they were promulgated with shocking disregard for the potential damages and death.

On the side of public health authorities, there was repeatedly an unpredictable debate.

On masks, the leading voice of U.S. public health has made a series of statements for months in direct contradiction to each other and to the data, and it still does not recognize the most compelling studies.

The most visible face of public health praised four northeastern U.S. states with the highest death rates for following his instructions despite their deadly performance.

Elite research universities, health agencies, and leading scientific journals quickly rallied to the gregarious thinking about the pandemic.

The priorities of teachers and their unions were unmasked as self-serving, driven by fear for the adult teachers, most of whom are at very low risk, at the expense of children's health and futures.

This would be tantamount to engaging in behavior designed to intimidate the speech that is essential to educating the public and obtaining the scientific truths we desperately need.

CHAPTER 1

America off the Rails

Because the country was not well prepared for a pandemic, one of the key tasks was to develop appropriate tests, the mainstay of public health in early infectious disease outbreaks.

Along with millions of Americans, I witnessed unprecedented responses from leaders and unscientific recommendations from public health advocates: societal lockdowns including business and school closing stores and schools, restriction of individuals' freedom of movement, and arbitrary orders from local, state, and federal governments.

In mid-March 2020, Ioannidis, who was virtually alone in the United States, warned with startling accuracy of the catastrophic health damage and devastating effects of widespread lockdown: "The additional deaths may not be due to the coronavirus, but to other widespread diseases and conditions such as heart attacks, strokes, trauma, hemorrhages, and others that are not adequately treated," and "we don't know how long social distancing and lockdowns measures can be sustained without serious economic, social and mental health consequences.

According to the Washington Post, Dr. Marc Lipsitch, professor of epidemiology at the Harvard T.H. Chan School of Public Health, said he was "stunned" by Ioannidis' trial.
If you divide the number of people who are going to die by the number of people who are infected, you get between three and five percent of people, which is very high.

At the same time, I have emphasized that the appropriate goal of public health policy is to minimize all harms, not simply to stop COVID-19 by all means.

Treating Covid-19 "at all costs" severely limits other medical care and instills fear in the public, leading to a massive health catastrophe, in addition to severe economic damage that could trigger a global poverty crisis of almost incalculable consequences.

We limited our study to a small data set on health care.
We wrote: "Considering only the loss of life due to lack of medical care and unemployment, which are solely attributable to the lockdown policy, we conservatively estimate that national lockdown is responsible for at least 700,000 lost life years per month, or about 1.5 million so far - already far exceeding the total COVID-19 figure.

"Later, Swedish health authorities reported that Sweden had opened daycare centers and schools for all 1.8 million children between the ages of one and 16 during the spring 2020 wave.

One of the fundamental obligations of anyone in a leadership role in public health was to consider all the potential harms of a policy, not just to try to prevent infection without considering other social costs.
Everyone who worked in medicine and public health knew that a nursing home was a real danger zone.

They needed someone who knew what they understood deep down: that the virus was serious and that some people were at high risk, but that the lockdown was a major mistake, an extremely destructive policy, an irrational overload on the public that had to be stopped.
The positions of these public health officials were at odds with new research and empirical evidence of the failure of their policy.

The proponents of lockdown, led by Dr. Fauci and Dr. Birx, were ignoring public health concerns as a whole and pushing for strict and unprecedented societal containment in order to stop COVID-19, a state-implemented policy that has caused untold harm and death, at all costs.

Almost every public health official who spoke in the media seemed to add to the fear and confusion.

CHAPTER 2

Off to Washington

It was John McEntee, from the Presidential Office Personnel Office, who I later learned was one of President Trump's closest associates.

"No, I didn't." "Did you make any negative comments in public, for example, on social media, and were you hostile to the president?" "No, I haven't." McEntee also asked who I advised during the 2016 campaign.
"Would you be willing to travel to Washington, D.C., to meet with the president?" he asked.

They expected me to be portrayed as a dissenter from Dr. Fauci and to become the scapegoat for those who hated the president.
Yet, no one could deny that being associated with President Trump was a considerable risk.

"What do you mean?" "You're going to meet the chief. You need a COVID test." McEntee accompanied me to the first floor of the EEOB, where I was tested.

The morning and early afternoon were filled with one-on-one meetings with the president's inner circle - Mark Meadows, Jared Kushner, Stephen Miller, Kayleigh McEnany, Marc Short, Vice President Pence, and others less known to the general public.

Meadows was the president's chief of staff, one of a series of chiefs under this president.

He was probably the determining factor in my being considered for the position of advisor to the president.

After my first meeting with Meadows, I ran into the vice president while being escorted to my next appointment.

"It's an honor to meet you, a great honor. Thank you so much for coming!" He told me that he was looking forward to meeting us later in the day.

The fact that the Vice President of the United States gave us such a warm welcome exceeded all expectations. After all, he was the president's most important and respected advisor and strategist on just about everything, as far as I could tell.

"Hi, nice to meet you. And you can call me Scott." "I'll call you Dr. Atlas. You've worked hard for this". And over the next four months, though we met several times each week, Kushner always used that formal title.

During a discussion about the pandemic, someone struts into the room with a printed draft of a tweet from the president ordering everyone to wear a mask.

"Well, that goes against what the president said about masks," I replied.

"Well," I replied cautiously, "I wouldn't want the President of the United States to say something that isn't scientifically incorrect, even if it's politically correct. And he has already made it known that he wears masks when appropriate, for example in crowded places. Shouldn't he be consistent?" My friend Rader, one of Jared's esteemed advisors, agreed with me emphatically.

I was then told it was time to meet with the president.

CHAPTER 3

Welcome to the West Wing

On my first visit to President Trump in the Oval Office, he and I discussed important issues surrounding the pandemic, with Jared Kushner and Johnny McEntee looking on.

In his office, we discussed the emerging role of the president's team.

The American people needed to hear from the president, and the president in turn needed advice and input on how to get his message out against the panic.

Yes, the president had initially endorsed the lockdowns the "Fifteen days to slow the spread" proposed by Fauci and Birx, even though he had major reservations.

"The President of the United States." After a short wait, a familiar voice came over the line.

"I thank you, Mr. President, for asking me to speak. I hope I can at least provide something useful to you and your team." During the conversation, he touched on various topics in passing.

At one point, he asked, "What about Fauci? Is it too late?" I replied, "Well, Mr. President, he's going to keep talking. He just recommended that everyone wear protective eyewear." Above all, the president's main point was that while the virus was very serious, continuing the lockdowns would shake people up, destroy the economy, keep kids out of school, and ruin small businesses.

According to what John said, "Derek must be persuaded. He has his doubts about the lockdowns, he's very analytical, and he's willing to understand the data behind your statements. You have to be able to convince him. Derek worked as the secretary to the president's staff.
It is true that the president explicitly agreed with my view that lockdowns were tremendously harmful to working families and children.

When I arrived, I was given an earlier draft of a grand strategy speech for President Trump to deliver and asked to revise it completely as soon as possible. I provided an overview of the latest knowledge about the virus, and then outlined a strategy focused on three points: enhanced protection for high-risk populations, careful monitoring of hospitals and intensive care units in every state, and guidance on the safe reopening of businesses, transportation, and schools.

The faces of the Task Force, Dr. Birx and Dr. Fauci, had silently watched the president's conjectures about the use of disinfectants and the effectiveness of various drugs, which was confusing and contributed to public confusion.

Although many people contributed to the president's comments, my contribution was required 24 hours a day and in real time.

My attendance was primarily intended to influence policy, not just to try to help the president and the country understand exactly what the current state of the pandemic was.

The president felt that the country needed to be reopened.

"A long-term nationwide shutdown is not sustainable and would inflict wide-ranging harm on the health and wellbeing of our inhabitants," their reopening guide declared in April 2020. Despite this, Dr. Birx, who represented the White House Task Force to governors and regional media while visiting states, ignored and openly contradicted the president's primary policy.

Any action on the ground was the responsibility of the governors, the chief executive of each state, not the president.

The vice president's task force also had an important leadership role that went beyond the logistics of producing and delivering aid.
It was a serious mistake to allow the national political message to be at odds with the message of the president of the United States.

CHAPTER 4

The Mad Hatter's Tea Party

After familiarizing myself with the surroundings of the West Wing, I attended the task force meetings in mid-August at Jared's direction.

My first observation about the task force was that the public perception was largely wrong, both in terms of its structure and operation.

The task force was led exclusively by Vice President Pence.

The president was not a member of the task force; in fact, and during my time in the White House, he never attended any of the sessions.

As far as I know, the president never spoke to the task force as a group during my four months in Washington.

If a member of the task force did not participate in a separate meeting with the president or attend the president's press briefings, he or she did not have direct contact with him either.

In practice, the task force's activities were multi-faceted: 1) medical-related assessments and advice; and 2) concrete deliverables, both in terms of production and logistics, including safety equipment, tests, emergency medical supplies, drugs, and vaccines.

The service delivery and operations part of the task force was working impressively, at least during the time I was there.

The medical part of the task force was a different story.

In her role as task force coordinator, she summarized the state of the pandemic for the vice president.

Those updates were occasionally sent to the Task Force and COVID Huddles, especially if there was an approaching event in those states.

Task Force meetings were held in the Situation Room.

Each Task Force meeting was held in the same room within the facility, with an overflow room nearby and videoconferencing connections to dozens more across the government.

Each task force meeting began with the distribution of handouts to all participants around the oval conference table, including the set agenda.

Dr. Birx was the nominal coordinator of the task force and always sat to the right of Vice President Pence, who sat at the head of the table.

The majority of the country, if not the whole world, assumed that Fauci held a leadership position on the Trump administration's task force.

The public assumption that Dr. Fauci had a leadership role in the task force itself could not have been more wrong.

Fauci had great public influence, but he was not responsible for anything specific within the Task Force.

Fauci provided the task force with information about the status of clinical trials enrollment, such as how many people in which demographic had been enrolled in vaccine or drug trials.

In addition to occasional updates on the status of enrollment in clinical trials, Fauci would occasionally provide the task force with a comment or update on the total number of participants in vaccine trials, usually when the vice president approached him with questions.

CHAPTER 5

The Politics of Testing

"Why are we testing healthy, younger people? Why don't we just test sick people?" he would ask.

Regardless, the answer to the failure, the available remedy for those who wanted to stop all cases, was more testing! Unbeknownst to the White House, several leading epidemiologists and infectious disease experts had opined that massive testing of healthy people in non-high-risk environments was not appropriate at this stage of the pandemic.

Sunetra Gupta of Oxford, a world-renowned epidemiologist, repeatedly emphasized that mass testing was illogical at this stage and that it was irrational to focus on cases that tested positive.

PCR tests detected virus fragments or dead virus in people who were not even contagious.

So 330 million each day, every fifteen minutes - might be enough to quell the testing frenzy! There would never be enough tests, no matter how many were conducted.

There were compelling reasons to test, important reasons to actually increase testing, but strategically.

To complicate matters, not only was Fauci-Birx's testing strategy unfocused, but their strategy bizarrely prioritized more testing in the lowest-risk people and in the lowest risk environments-students and schools-while allowing deaths to continue in nursing homes and assisted-living facilities, where it was assumed that once-a-week testing was effective.

The obsession with testing everyone, everywhere, all the time, including low-risk people in low-risk settings, was wrong, illogical, and harmful.

The irony was that, almost everyone thought the president was simply looking for an excuse to cover up "insufficient" testing capacity, when there were valid reasons to use testing in an entirely different way to maximize its benefits.

It reminded me of Catch-22, when 150 million antigen tests became available weeks later, I was asked by several people in the COVID Huddle: "Now that we have these tests, what are we going to do with them?"

For the first few days and even after, I would meet with John Rader at lunch over cookies and cappuccino in his small office in the West Wing.

I talked about priority testing of all residents of nursing homes and long-term care facilities, which should be done at least twice a week; testing of all nursing home workers, which should be done at least twice a week, with this frequency to be increased to daily in high-infectivity areas; priority testing of all asymptomatic high-risk persons known to be at risk; priority screening of all symptomatic high-risk persons to protect their older social groups; proactive notification and strict ASPR protection of all high-risk persons in the medical sector in areas of increased community activity who bring COVID-like illnesses to emergency rooms; and if they are known to have been exposed, ensuring that they are also tested.

The most crucial improvements were highlighted by Giroir, all of which had already been agreed upon by every doctor on the Task Force, as well as those at the CDC, FDA, and HHS. Both Redfield and Giroir stressed to the group that the decision to test was now even more clearly in the hands of both the individual and their doctor, implying that a physician was now more involved in the decision to test.

He explained that all testing opportunities were still available to anyone who wished to take one.

If a person has only mild symptoms, they should isolate themselves and take extra precautions to protect everyone at risk in the house, but they don't necessarily need a test because a test would not change their treatment.

Birx explained the importance of testing asymptomatic people as well.

Are these politicians our leaders? The people in charge of the United States of America? Many friends from abroad - from Switzerland, France, and even Brazil - emailed me asking, "What the hell is wrong with the United States?" Redfield first defended his new guidelines in a written statement that was widely reported: "Anyone who needs a COVID-19 test, can get one.

Not everyone who wants a test needs one; the key is to involve the necessary public health community in the decision and take appropriate follow-up action.

Instead, protect the weakest. These two world-class viruses and testing experts praised the appropriateness, logic, and science - the accuracy - of the new testing protocols: "The new CDC guidelines appropriately focus testing resources on hospital staff and the older generation.

With the new CDC guidelines, strategic, age-targeted viral testing will protect the elderly from lethal exposure to Covid-19 and children and young adults from unnecessary school closures.

CHAPTER 6

My Role as the President's Advisor

Being a runaway also meant that my motivation as an advisor to the president was different.

Despite the many brains in the president's inner circle, no one mentioned the most obvious fact of all: lockdowns did not prevent the elderly from dying, even though it was known from the start who the most vulnerable were.

Initially, the remarks that the chair was to read were distributed to several people for their input.

The president needed to reiterate these facts and not let the fear-obsessed media and power-hungry lockdown advocates entertain the myth that there was a clear choice between saving the economy and saving human lives.

In nearly every briefing or speech from August onward, the president provided specific data that updated the public on trends in problematic parts of the country; he reminded people to take the usual precautions; he stressed the importance of opening up schools and society while carefully protecting the elderly ; he put into perspective how the entire world was struggling to limit the damage of the pandemic; and he said very directly something that almost no one seemed to understand, including some members of the White House task force - that locking down society would not eliminate or eradicate the virus.

I quickly felt that going into Brady's press room was tantamount to a fight, one that I profoundly despised.
On one occasion, after the usual preliminary meeting in the Oval Office and review of the script and topics to be covered, Kayleigh showed the president the new seating chart for the day.

Before entering the Oval Office, Kayleigh McEnany and I had a private press briefing conversation with President Trump.
President Trump listened intently and nodded, as if he intended to take her advice.
As usual, the President made most, if not all, of the remarks he had on file, occasionally looking over to me and making passing comments.

President Trump dominated the press conference, while I sat in a chair next to Larry Kudlow and Secretary Steve Mnuchin, ready to take questions.

To my amazement, President Trump immediately pointed directly at the first reporter Kayleigh had warned him to skip.

The reporter asked some innocuous questions to which the president responded aggressively by denying the premise.

After the president was escorted out, we all followed, not knowing why.

Someone approached the president and asked if he was okay.

The president looked around and said, "Sure, look around, there's no safer place," pointing out the impressive security personnel who had come so quickly to protect him.

President Trump said, "OK, let's go," and we all walked back into the room, with the president leading the way.

COVID testing was necessary for anyone meeting with the president or vice president that day.

If the president asked me a question, I gave him my honest opinion.

Dr. Birx and I were both present at only one or two of the Oval Office briefings I attended in early August to answer questions or explain key topics for the president.

In the Oval Office, I sat in the row of chairs in front of President Trump with HHS Advisor Paul Mango, General Gus Perna, and Moncef Slaoui - three key members of Operation Warp Speed - while President Trump held court.

At a memorable preliminary meeting in August, Birx and I were both seated in front of the president, in an arc of four or five chairs arranged in front of his desk.
No one was surprised when the president brought up one of his favorite topics: testing.

CHAPTER 7

Meet the Press!

As I treated each request as urgent and in real time, I felt extra pressure; but nothing was more urgent than reviewing the president's public remarks.

Adding to the requirement for my input was that this president loved engaging with the press.

My introduction to the press by the president was spontaneous and totally unexpected.

The first few days after I arrived, I was not yet involved in the "pre-briefing" that took place before the president entered the Brady Press Briefing Room to make his statements.

A small but changing group of relevant advisors accompanied the president into the Oval Office.

Typically, Kayleigh, Stephen Miller, Kushner, Derek Lyons, Hope Hicks, and a few others would stand or sit while the president went over the script and hand-edited what he wanted to use as his script.

"Excuse me, Mr. President." "Good morning, Scott!" he smiled broadly as he held his annotation notebook in his hand.

"What mistake?" "The sentence in there now says 'without an increase in deaths,' but it should say 'without a significant increase in deaths.' That's not the same thing." President Trump looked around, apparently surprised that I was interested in this trivial detail.
Jared smiled, shrugged his shoulders, and said, "All right, let's go. Good luck!" The president, Kayleigh, and I headed toward the entrance.

On my first appearance in the Brady press room, the president answered questions while I looked on next to Kayleigh McEnany.

My revelation in the briefing room came out very awkwardly, with only an incidental remark from the president at the podium.

"Everyone knows Scott Atlas, right? Scott is a very famous man, who is also very well respected," President Trump said.

Without the unforgettable support of two extraordinary, truly extraordinary people - the phenomenal Liz Horning, senior advisor to the president, and a brilliant senior advisor to a prominent governor - I would have been pretty much on my own.

Two conflicting messages were sent out: The Task Force was insisting on lockdowns the Birx-Fauci facility, while the president was simultaneously insisting on reopening it.

I assumed that the White House team understood that if I was delegitimized, the president would be undermined as well.

Everyone had warned me that anyone who sided with the president would be attacked, but the relentlessness still surprised me.

Arbitrary distortions and lies aimed at destroying anyone who answered the president's call to help the country were now quite acceptable.

And why? Because I had the boldness to step forward and help the country alongside a president the media despised.

When Fox News' Chris Wallace heard my clinical opinion that we expected the president to recover from COVID and return to work soon, he told his Fox colleague, "He's not an epidemiologist!" As if an epidemiologist's opinion on a clinical medical issue is more credible than that of a doctor with decades of experience seeing thousands of patients with infectious and other diseases in the United States and around the world.

In September 2020, shortly after I was publicly introduced as an advisor to the president, a group of Stanford Medical School professors published a letter containing several false claims about my policy views.

CHAPTER 8

Early Conflicts with the Task Force

All through the spring and into summer, Drs. Birx and Fauci represented the Task Force, both in the Oval Office and to the public in the media.

Rolling lockdowns, as advocated by Birx and Fauci, were implemented in nearly all states.

Regardless of what the president said about the need to reopen, almost all states followed Fauci and Birx's recommendations, with a handful of exceptions, such as South Dakota, Florida, and a few others.

The president had clearly stated his policy on masks - recommending them when social distancing was not possible, as NIH, WHO and others did; Birx, Fauci and Redfield consistently insisted in interviews and with governors that masks were required across the board, if not prescribed for everyone.

Regardless of what the president himself said, the vice president and the political staff - indeed, almost everyone - feared Fauci and Birx, who enjoyed a very high public profile.

The perception of Fauci and Birx by the voters captured the messages of the administration - except for the president himself, who in all his statements continued to emphasize reopening with targeted protection of the weakest.

The more Fauci and Birx contradicted the president's ideas, the more they were picked up by the anti-Trump media and used to justify draconian executive orders by governors and local health officials.

If Birx and Fauci were ignoring all the data that went against their policies, including months of experience around the world, why should they suddenly reconsider everything? Why would they listen to me, an outsider? In the middle of the first task force meeting in mid-August, I realized that my assumptions were correct-my participation in the task force would do no good.

These valuable ties continued while I was in the White House, providing me with data completely unknown to Birx and the other task force members.

The first item on the task force agenda was nearly always an update by Birx on the data and on her travels. As far as I know, Dr. Birx himself composed documents for each state, which were assumed to reflect the advice of the task force.

Dr. Birx began talking about "The Sunbelt"-particularly Arizona-by saying, "We've got the cases down there." Echoing statements in the July 20 email that I had received weeks earlier, she said that Arizona had proven that certain closures, such as closing bars and restricting eating inside restaurants, as well as introducing mask requirements, worked.

Birx then insisted that the same restrictions be introduced everywhere, including closing bars, limiting restaurant hours of operation, and mask mandate.
Dr. Birx evidently didn't understand that reported dates on most government agency dashboards and in the media at the time, such as the COVID Tracking Project, were misstating actual event dates even after more than six months of looking at the figures every day.

Again, Birx said nothing about the antibody data, nor did Fauci or Redfield.

While Birx, Fauci, and Redfield focused exclusively on stopping cases at all costs in their media interviews and advice to governors, pushing their brain-numbing message of "Wash your hands, stay away from others, wear masks" message, I was the only doctor representing the White House who also explained to the public that the lockdowns were destroying people, providing data in written pieces, interviews, and through the president's remarks.

As always, Dr. Birx provided his current data - numbers, trends, and some anecdotes from the street. As always, Dr. Birx added her color-coded tables of numbers, which she had gathered in a stack of charts and tables already distributed to everyone in attendance.

Birx provided fresh updates on cases, hospitalizations, and deaths, which kicked off the typical conversation.
As is often the case, Fauci spoke in support of Dr. Birx's worries. He stated that people needed to be even more warned about the dangers of the spread of the virus, as well as the importance of wearing masks and keeping a safe distance.

CHAPTER 9

Debating "the Science" about Schools

The CDC had admitted that "[COVID] deaths in children are lower than in each of the last five influenza seasons" and that "among children, cumulative COVID-19 hospitalization rates are lower than cumulative hospitalization rates for influenza in recent influenza seasons." This is the conclusion of a study of North American pediatric hospitals published in JAMA Pediatrics: "Our data indicate that the risk of critical illness in children is much higher for influenza than for COVID-19." The month before I arrived, the president and the administration had pushed for schools to reopen.

Everyone who bothered to check also knew that it was extremely detrimental to children.

Worse, it was common knowledge that closing the schools was particularly destructive to working-class and poor children.

Children who depended on schools for nutritional need or to know if they needed glasses or a hearing aids were now ignored.

The number of reported cases of child abuse dropped rapidly - hundreds of thousands during the spring 2020 school closures alone - because schools are the first place where such abuse is found.

Given the enormous social harm caused by the school closures, the icing on the cake was that child abuse hardly transmitted to adults.

Studies from Finland, Sweden, the Netherlands, Switzerland, France, the United Kingdom, and other countries confirmed that children were almost always infected from adults, not the other way around; that few cases occurred in schools; that teachers did not have higher rates of infection than other occupational groups; and that "outbreaks" in schools were usually just positive tests without symptoms or mild illnesses.

He added that even if children were transmitting it to the adults, which was not a reason to close schools.

Even several teachers and school board members reached out to me, stunned at how schools were shut down and unsure what to do.

The statement was reported by Reuters, and the first sentence revealed the obsession with masks that had taken over the entire pandemic narrative: "U.S. President Donald Trump on Wednesday issued eight recommendations for reopening U.S. schools in the midst of the coronavirus pandemic, including the recommendation to use masks when social distancing is not possible." The event took place on the same day and was a follow-up to the Vice President's roundtable discussion with South Carolina Governor McMaster three weeks earlier on reopening schools.

The President, Vice President, Secretary DeVos, and several invited parents, teachers, and outside experts spoke about the urgent need to get children back in school.

One education policy expert, Paul Peterson, director of the Program on Education Policy and Governance at Harvard University, explained the consequences of preventing children from attending school.
Almost all school districts implemented a policy of closing in-person schools in the late spring, based on fear and directly contradicting the evidence.

Even after the excellent CDC publication of July 23, 2020, which recognized the importance of private school openings and the damage caused by school closures, the task force, particularly Birx, but also Redfield and Fauci, insisted that we must redouble school testing, quarantine, and extensive efforts to contain the disease, even in young children - even though we know they interfere with learning and normal socialization.

The most significant difference between a school and the rest of the world was that schools were lower-risk environments, less dangerous than the surrounding neighborhood.

"There is very little indication that the virus is transmitted" in schools, according to one of the world's largest studies on coronavirus in schools, which involved one hundred institutions in the United Kingdom.

CHAPTER 10

The Talented Dr. Redfield

One day in mid-September, I was munching on my daily cookie in Rader's cramped office while watching Dr. Robert Redfield, the CDC director, testify before Congress.

A week earlier, the country had witnessed Redfield's bizarre testimony on masks, which contained some of the most ignorant comments imaginable from someone who claims to be a scientist, let alone an incumbent in one of the most influential public health positions in the country.

Redfield's statements simultaneously shattered faith in the upcoming, very efficient vaccine while exaggerating the elderly's risk tolerance through the use of masks.

I remember two recognized scientific colleagues asking me on the same day, "What the hell is Redfield talking about?" Redfield was also quoted as saying that Americans might not have access to a vaccine until "deep into 2021."

Ironically, a few days later, Redfield was overheard by a reporter on a flight saying "Everything Scott Atlas says is wrong." By revealing to the press the disagreements within the Task Force, he undermined the government and the press took up the issue.

Redfield had been exposed in the Task Force meetings since I came on board.

As director of the CDC, Redfield had a lot of credibility, so his statements questioning the vaccine and its timing were important to the United States and the world.

"I can only rely on what I was told. I didn't want to attribute motivation to Redfield's words; even now, when I know that vaccinations will begin in December 2020, exactly as we had planned in the HHS schedules, I don't understand why he said that.

I tried my hardest to cover for Redfield, but I had no choice but to be honest.

"I seriously doubt Dr. Redfield believes that," he said. "He spoke very consciously," McCallum noted, breaking in.

"We all make missteps when we speak." Redfield's statement before Congress on September 23 immediately caught my attention.

I couldn't believe it when Redfield informed Congress that "more than 90% of the population"—more than 300 million individuals in the US—remains vulnerable to the disease.

Redfield's primary claim was wrong from the start.

The flaws in Redfield's estimate were more profound.

Because T-cells are apparently not detected by antibody tests, these people were not included in Redfield's count. A legal advisor to the president warned me with a smile on his face, "Scott, don't just say bluntly, 'Redfield is wrong! Say something softer, like, 'He misrepresented things.'" I nodded, knowing I had to hold my words back, even though this was the same man who had tried to destroy me in the national press just days before.

An ABC News reporter asked me directly if Redfield's claim that more than 90 percent of Americans were vulnerable to the disease was true.

"Is Redfield political or just stupid?" he asked, shaking his head quietly. I looked directly at the president and hesitated.

Needless to say, the media immediately seized on the difference of opinion between Redfield and me.

It was part of the presentation of the conflict between me and the other Task Force doctors, a conflict that Redfield had personally provoked by insultingly and unjustifiably saying that everything I had said was "False." Later, Dr. Fauci appeared on television and criticized my direct attempt to clarify important information as "extraordinarily inappropriate." I wondered if he was more concerned with protecting the reputation of his fellow bureaucrat and undermining mine than with ensuring that correct information was made available to the American public.

CHAPTER 11

"Don't Rock the Boat!"

The Task Force failed to conduct the necessary tests very early in the pandemic, before the infection had spread so widely.

His advice for more general public duties and restrictions, more quarantines, and more social lockdowns was not just given orally during its dozens of visits to local officials, university administrators, and governors.

Dr. Birx spoke about mandates and lockdowns as the White House Coronavirus Task Force's traveling representative, even though her statements clearly contradicted those of the president of the United States. Giroir stated they couldn't do anymore because they'd developed and deployed a massive testing capability; I agreed that they had indeed developed the testing capability.

Dr. Birx agreed and tried to refute the whole idea of offering more protection to those at risk of death.

Why nursing home staff were only tested once a week? We all knew that cases in nursing homes were almost always introduced by staff.

Many staff worked in more than one nursing home, which meant we were testing an incredibly high-risk group.

Why did we make the same general testing recommendation for all nursing homes? Shouldn't we have quickly increased the number of tests if there were more cases in the surrounding community where the employees lived? We were already tracking COVID visits to the ER in the communities.

Why were we ignoring the elderly who lived alone or in the community and were exposed to the disease when they congregated in senior centers where they were not screened? No, I insisted, much more could be done.

We worked together to develop a set of refined guidelines for nursing homes and together recommended that point-of-care testing be done much more frequently in nursing homes.

We emphasized the importance of increasing the frequency of testing by staff to three times a week or more when the prevalence in the community is high.

We added the criterion "COVID-like illness in the emergency department" to determine the rate of infection in the community, as this is simpler, already tabulated everywhere, and does not suffer from the arbitrariness of testing.

CHAPTER 12
Inside the COVID Huddle

In addition to Kushner, Adam Boehler, Birx, and their collaborators, a large and very diverse group participated in COVID meetings, later called "China Virus Huddles" on the printed agendas.

Task Force meetings were largely about operational updates, but medical discussions were never directly on the president's radar.

It was from Birx's descriptions and warnings of mass deaths if no lockdowns were put in place that reactions occurred, such as the emphasis on increased testing of healthy, low-risk students and the planning of events at the White House and on the street. Few people questioned Dr. Birx's claims at the COVID Huddles, mainly because virtually no one in the room had a medical or scientific background.

Almost no one in the COVID Huddle really understood that Birx's tactic was not just a failure to stop cases - it was far worse than that.

Another strangeness of the situation was that the Birx lockdowns directly contradicted the president's stated strategy of reopening schools and society while focusing on safeguarding the most vulnerable.

The common theme I heard in the three months leading up to the election was purely political - they didn't want to "Rock the boat." They said they were afraid of "upsetting" Birx because she had great public prestige and "we were so close to an election," as Meadows and others kept reminding me.

At these sessions, the majority of participants said nothing regarding the conclusions that led to Birx's policy.

Birx was under the orders of the Vice President, not Kushner or anyone else.

The measures recommended by Birx and Fauci were implemented by almost every state, and these measures were empirically unsuccessful.

Regardless of my presence in the press briefings, at the contentious Task Force meetings, or at the COVID Huddles, Birx remained the main advisor and the only Task Force representative to governors.

To complicate matters, Birx used circular reasoning as "proof" that locking down had successfully stopped the spread of cases.

I kept insisting that it was important to tell the American public the truth and that the president's statements should reflect accurate data, even though I could not reach Birx and the task force.

With a few exceptions, the nation implemented exactly what Birx and Fauci and the Task Force had recommended.

After sitting in on Task Force meetings and hearing COVID Huddles, I was ecstatic, almost astonished, when someone approached me and told me they agreed with me.

To be a member of that Task Force, to listen to these so-called experts wielding such power, individuals who denied the data and didn't even question the scientific literature.

"With a cycle threshold of 35 or more, the chances of this being replicable [contagious] are slim to none... It has to be said that these are just dead nucleotides, period."

Yet the White House Task Force doctors who sat for months in the Situation Room-Birx, Fauci, Giroir, Redfield literally never discussed this critical error in the meetings I attended in Washington.

The inexplicable lack of critical thinking among the task force physicians, even after nine months, was brought home to me in late September, when the vice president asked me to prepare a presentation on testing for the task force.

The task force still did not have complete and comprehensive knowledge of something so fundamental? I had no desire to prepare this useless report, but I politely replied "fine" to the vice president's request.

CHAPTER 13

POTUS Meets the Real Experts...in Secret

The president needed to know as soon as possible that some of the country's top experts disagreed with Dr. Birx's suggestions, and that the facts supported his reasonable idea that the lockdowns were destroying the country.

Above all, Dr. Birx seems to enjoy working with the Vice President.

Since the President did not attend a single meeting of the working group, it is possible that her counsel did not reach him regularly.

The Vice President must have realized that the President's views on reopening were at odds with the advice from the task force.

I approached my Stanford colleague Jay Bhattacharya, an infectious disease, health policy, and economics expert, in early August and told him I wanted to arrange a private roundtable meeting with the president.

The roundtable was canceled three hours later by the vice president's scheduling office via email.
The information needed to be heard by the President and Vice President, even if it made people uncomfortable.

The background discussion would take place tomorrow with the Vice President, the leader of the Task Force.
Each time the president was introduced, he nodded, smiled, and said, "Thank you very much. Thank you very much for coming." Then, looking from one visitor to another, then around the room, at his advisors, both on the sidelines and behind us on the couches, he exclaimed, "We have five geniuses here!" The president was pumped, and I was relieved that we had made the right choice.

President Trump listened closely to Dr. Joe Ladapo during our private discussion with leading physicians and scientists in the Oval Office.

At another meeting, the president began discussing taxes with Treasury Secretary Steven Mnuchin, and I happened to be in the room.

"Mr. President, we really need to move on," Meadows finally remarked as he moved forward. The president, as he regularly did with guests, asked each of the invited doctors to pose with him behind the Resolute Desk for a portrait.
Jay instantly retrieved a chart he had created illustrating CDC trends, which the president had shown during a recent press briefing, and had it autographed at his desk.
As the meeting with the invited medical scientists approached, I prepared Vice President Pence in the hallway upstairs in the West Wing with my folder full of journal articles.

In the Roosevelt Room of the West Wing, Vice President Pence presided over the meeting with the group of medical scientists.

Who in their right mind would not agree with this approach? Wasn't it to refute the false claim that this President, this Vice President, had not "listened to the science"? Instead, the decision was just the opposite.

CHAPTER 14

Rebutting the Science Deniers

Irrespective of how ridiculous the personal assaults were, I was very concerned that the media's attack on me was damaging the credibility of my message.
I recommended to Martin that we organize a high-profile panel discussion in front of the Washington media to demonstrate to the world that epidemiologists and infectious disease experts agreed with the method I was suggesting.

She too had been pilloried by the media in the UK. Somehow, her official title of "Theoretical epidemiologist" disqualified her from expressing her opinion, even though she was one of the world's leading authorities in the field of infectious disease epidemiology and immunology and had, among other things, developed a clinical influenza vaccine that could eliminate the need for a new influenza vaccine each year.

In order to get as much media coverage as possible, I initially hoped to invite all participants to a meeting with the president, but that idea was later taken off the table - not only because of the political sensitivities of all participants, but also because I didn't want the event to be politicized and therefore delegitimized.

The media was hostile to any opinion that went against the accepted narrative. Even some of those who had published my opinions and had had incredible success in attracting viewers were now reluctant and unfortunately giving in to anti-Trump pressure.

I spoke with Azar staff about organizing media coverage, including a press release - everything was ready, they assured me.

The media buzz was palpable, as was the anxiety in the West Wing, and the communications team was of course completely overwhelmed.
I couldn't wait to see the media coverage as soon as the photos and official press release announced the procedure.
Martin was scheduled to leave in the afternoon to join his family, but Jay and Sunetra would join me at my hotel that evening for a celebratory dinner.
We talked about the lockdowns, the distortions in the media, and the shocking lack of critical thinking by government officials and scientists around the world.
We discussed about the malicious hostility, not only from the media, but also from our academic colleagues in the United States and the United Kingdom. In the middle of dinner, I suddenly remembered the BBC interview.

After months of giving the floor to experts who were asserting the need for lockdowns with no other opinion in sight, the BBC was now saying that they would only interview Sunetra, Martin, and Jay if experts on "the other side of the argument" were also included.

Then came the time for the interview with Laura Ingraham, with Jay and Sunetra sitting side by side, while Martin was connected from Boston.

CHAPTER 15

POTUS Gets COVID

Early in the morning of Friday, October 2, while I was arranging the details of the trio of epidemiologists' visit to Washington, D.C., I learned that the president had tested positive for COVID and had been taken to Walter Reed for treatment.

The president himself broke the news in his usual way - on Twitter.

At the same time, I was confident in the outcome, as the president was in relatively good health - sure, overweight and older, but I had never seen anyone with more energy and vitality at that age.

As a result, I gave the reporter a very simple statement: the president was a strong, healthy man, and although he was an older citizen, we expected him to recover well and return to work.

No impartial individual who has ever spent time with President Trump would conclude that he is anything less than a vigorous, enthusiastic man—the polar opposite of feeble.

Several other people in the West Wing kept asking me to speak to reporters because I was the only clinically experienced physician on the entire team who was not one of his doctors, because I was in a position to talk about COVID, and because I was specifically the president's advisor on this subject.

"Hello, Mr. President, how are you feeling?" "I'm feeling great! I want to get out of here!" he thundered.

Like most irrational behavior during the pandemic, virtually everyone in the West Wing was then tested, regardless of whether they were in close proximity to the president.

On the same Saturday morning phone call, President Trump gave abrupt instructions, "Tell everyone there, call Jason, no new tweets, tell Kayleigh nothing has changed. No requirement to wear a mask, it's still 'masks only if you can't maintain a social distance,' as always. No requirement to wear a mask in the West Wing, nothing has changed, absolutely nothing." Then he exclaims, irritated: ""Where the hell is everyone? Where are the interviews, I don't see anyone on TV"? Dr. Fauci, of course, continued to interview and present the ubiquitous and potentially negative turn of events, which never happened.

As I ate breakfast at my table in the lobby of the Trump Hotel, I couldn't help but follow the breathless reporting on the four big screen TVs. The next day, I wasn't the least bit shocked to see the president greeting his supporters from the back of the limousine as it circled the hospital.

As usual, all the reporters and anchors had suddenly become pundits, taking exception to the president's every action.

CHAPTER 16

The Election Approaches

I screamed, completely furious, "Lockdowns are defined in this way! Stating "I'm against lockdowns" and then recommending policies that result in lockdowns is the same as saying "I'm for lockdowns!"
One of the usual agenda items for the COVID huddle was an update on vaccine development.

At one huddle, a few weeks before the elections, it was decided to announce the success of the vaccine development as soon as the data would be known and disclosed.

Everyone had already witnessed several interviews in which officials inside and outside the government had expressed doubt that vaccine development would be possible by the end of the year.

What's to stop you? Because Stephen Hahn and the FDA suddenly added a sixty-day gap between the doses being administered to half of the test subjects and a safety assessment of the mRNA vaccines in trials.

Delaying a life-saving vaccine for political reasons seems almost inconceivable, but we had already seen inexcusable and obviously political comments by our key politicians that likely cost lives.
It is clear that no one could see the efficacy data until it was reviewed by the outside expert panel, the Data and Safety Management Board, but that initial review had to take place before the elections.

It was also clear to all that just the evidence of the vaccine's success would be a great news, even if the final evaluation came later, and that it would likely boost the President's chances.

I replied, "Wait a minute, Paul and I just looked at the numbers; those numbers match exactly what's in the agreements!" But Birx continued to denounce the estimates, shaking her head. I wondered, "Why on earth would she doubt numbers that come directly from the original documents?" Downplaying the near-term availability of the vaccine would prevent positive information from being released before the election, whether politics is the motivation or not.

According to Stat News, William Gruber, Pfizer's vice president for clinical research and vaccine development, said the decision was made not to analyze the 32 cases. He answered press questions about the vaccine from the podium while Moncef Slaoui, head of vaccine development at OWS, and President Trump looked on.

CHAPTER 17
The Florida Success Story

DeSantis asked if I would come to Florida and tour his state during one of these calls in August.

Meanwhile, the Trump administration had established a good partnership with the state of Florida, providing economic help, support for school reopening, medical supplies, technical assistance and staff.

The White House arranged the details of my trip in coordination with the governor's team in Florida.
We hosted a roundtable discussion and press conference where Florida's chief education officer, a parent, and others spoke about the progress and success of reopening of schools in Florida nationwide.

The press conference at The Villages began with a new data presentation by Governor DeSantis - he reviewed numbers showing Florida's trends in cases, hospitalizations, ICU and hospital bed occupancy and community infection rates.

Commissioner of Education Corcoran emphasized the significance of in-person learning, stating that all of Florida's school districts have been opened and that over one million students are already enrolled in in-person classes.

Florida's schools opened in August 2020 and remained open throughout the year.
While the vast majority of states imposed and maintained strict societal restrictions, Florida opened its amusement parks, universities, and businesses, and ended its mask mandates.

The lockdown states have caused significant damage, both physical and psychological, that will last for decades, while Florida has avoided that damage.

After a full year, we know the answer to the question about Florida - the only major state to implement a targeted protection strategy, the only large state I personally advised during the pandemic that rejected the Birx-Fauci strategy: Florida outperformed the national average and outperformed more than half of our states in terms of COVID deaths per capita.

Florida led the ten largest states in the lowest percentage increase in excess mortality during the pandemic, a percentage that includes deaths due to the virus and the lockdown, the most valid epidemiological statistic for comparing deaths during the pandemic; Florida beat forty states in age-adjusted COVID death rate for the population at risk and also beat about the same number of states for all age groups.

Florida had an age-adjusted mortality rate for the elderly and for all residents that was 40% lower than that of the United States as a whole.

Florida outperformed California, which had a younger population, in virtually every meaningful way. This is an important comparison because these are such diverse states with relatively similar climates, with one dramatic difference: the governor of California imposed and enforced strict lockdowns, whereas the governor of Florida opened his state in the summer.

Florida outperformed California by 30 percent in age-adjusted COVID mortality among those over sixty-five, by 40 percent in age-adjusted COVID mortality among those under sixty-five, and by nearly 60 percent in percentage of excess mortality during the pandemic.

Unlike nearly every other governor, Governor DeSantis established the right policy almost a year ago, offering targeted protection to Floridians while opening schools and businesses in Florida.

CHAPTER 18

Speaking the Truth to the End

In my opinion, this delay, due to a series of subtle and not-so-subtle maneuvers on the part of the president's opponents, is one of the most heinous accusations against the moral vacuum that I witnessed during my time in Washington.

People were apparently so obsessed with their desire to prevent this president's re-election that they didn't care if people died because of the delay in vaccine approval. For me personally, the president's defeat did not change anything.

My position as an advisor to the president was limited to 130 days appointment, so no matter who won the election, I was already on my way out of Washington.

In an effort to help, I had carefully considered who would be best suited to fill these key positions if the president won re-election.

As Thanksgiving neared in mid-November, I decided to ask the president to approve my plans to return to California to be with my family.

Objective journalism in America was dead. Added to that was the high-profile criticism from a group of uninformed and dishonest Stanford professors blinded by their hatred of President Trump.

They were in a state of fear when I appeared as the president's counselor.

On November 19, 2020, the Stanford Faculty Senate issued a resolution condemning my work as an advisor to the president.

After reflecting on the situation and realizing that my term was coming to an end, I decided to call the president.

"Hello, Scott! How are you?" It was the president.

"Good morning, Mr. President. I'm doing well. I hope you are, too. I didn't want to waste time and continued.

The president's closest advisors, including the vice president, seemed more concerned with politics, even though the task force was giving bad advice that went against the president's desire to reopen schools and businesses.

They prevented the president from separating himself from people who were grossly incompetent, and only because of the election, simply because these high-profile bureaucrats were seen in a positive light by the public.

"Well, Mr. President, I will say this. You've got guts. I have guts. But the people closest to you - they didn't have any. They didn't have guts. They let you down. ." I was expecting pushback, but I didn't get any.

CHAPTER 19

Assessing the Trump Pandemic Response

As time went on, like many scientists and health policy scholars, I absorbed new information and aggregated the most recent data from around the world in order to offer the president and the nation with the most up-to-date information for the greater benefit.

Based on their assumptions about me, they thought I wanted to defend the president and his administration's handling of the pandemic.

Since his statement on March 23, 2020, during the initial 15-day lockdown that "the cure can't be worse than the problem," President Trump has repeatedly outlined his overall strategy: Protect the vulnerable, avoid overcrowding in hospitals, and open schools and businesses.

These principles were reiterated throughout the pandemic in the president's speeches, briefings and statements inside and outside the White House.

The task force was called "The White House Coronavirus Task Force," but it was not in synch President Trump.
The President's Action and Inaction Assigning roles in the pandemic by level of government is a bit more complicated than a simple division of responsibility, since the president is himself, by definition, the nation's highest executive official.

The perceived authorities - yes, the decision makers - were the president's advisers, Anthony Fauci and Deborah Birx.
Between spring 2020 and the election, the president mentioned focused protection and reopening more than a dozen times.

The Birx-Fauci policies was not only in direct contradiction to the president's statements, it also resulted in the deaths of people.
The apparent divergence between what Fauci and Birx were advising and what the president himself was advocating resulted in chaotic and mixed messages from the White House.
Clearly, the largest part of the president's failure was undoubtedly the fact that he did not change his task force.
Between spring 2020 and the election, the president mentioned focused protection and reopening more than a dozen times.

The Birx-Fauci policies were not only in direct contradiction to the president's statements but also resulted in the deaths of people.

The apparent divergence between what Fauci and Birx were advising and what the president himself was advocating resulted in chaotic and mixed messages from the White House.

Clearly, the largest part of the president's failure was undoubtedly the fact that he did not change his task force.

None were made; it remained intact until the end of the president's term.
We all saw how many people in the media praised Dr. Fauci and Dr. Birx precisely because of their differences with the president.

Perhaps because of the inconsistencies and misstatements at the podium, it appeared that the president had decided to be less visible and delegate to state governors what they had all requested: administration of their local pandemic.

The president's personal participation in enlightening the public and showing the requisite expertise and attention to detail contributed to the success of the campaign.

The Trump Administration's Reaction Despite enabling the Task Force to continue advocating for ill-advised lockdowns, the president directed a number of crucial and very successful policies that altered the course of the pandemic and saved lives.

To any objective observer, the president and his administration have a long list of concrete successes to their credit: He stopped incoming air travel from China and Europe long before any other country, despite the opposition of task force officials at the time.

Paul Mango, Secretary Azar's senior advisor, kept me updated every step of the process, ensuring that I never misspoke or gave the president of the United States any false information regarding vaccines or pharmaceuticals under OWS. Many of the Trump administration's actions and reputation will surely be slandered in history, but it will be tough to dismiss the accomplishments of Operation Warp Speed.

CHAPTER 20

And That's the Science!

The painful truth about masks in many ways, there is nothing more representative of the SARS2 coronavirus pandemic than masks.

Dr. Fauci, in his publicly available e-mail to Sylvia Burwell, former secretary of the Department of HHS, explained the reality to his former colleague: "The typical mask you buy at the drugstore is not really effective in preventing a sufficiently small virus from passing through the material. It may offer a small advantage in preventing large droplets from escaping if someone coughs or sneezes on you." The SARS2 virus measures about 0.12 micrometers, which is similar to the flu virus and much smaller than the pore size of surgical masks.

I opposed mask mandates that required everyone in society to wear a mask for a variety of reasons.

My words echoed those of the Harvard Medical School writers of the New England Journal of Medicine article "Universal Masking in Hospitals in the Covid-19 Era," which is highlighted at the top of that page: "On June 3, 2020, the authors of this article state, "We strongly support the calls of public health agencies for all individuals to wear masks when circumstances require them to remain within 6 feet of others for an extended period of time.

The empirical evidence from the US and all over the world already had shown masks failed to stop COVID-19 cases from surging.

Relying on masks would be dangerous because it would imply protection for those at risk of death, such as the elderly, without legitimate protection.

"In June 2021, JAMA Pediatrics finally called public attention to the dangers of masks in children; even wearing masks for a short period of time revealed harmful accumulations of carbon dioxide.

Masks impede communication and create a poor learning environment in school; bacterial contamination occurs, especially when worn for extended periods; masks cause eye and skin infections.

Is there anyone who honestly believe that the psychological development of children is not be affected after they have been instilled with the idea that everyone, including themselves, is a constant danger to everyone else? Let's take a look at what scientists knew in the spring and summer of 2020: in April 2020, the New England Journal of Medicine published a study on universal masking for healthcare personnel.

The Harvard Medical School authors began by stating what was known: "We know that wearing a mask outside of healthcare facilities, if any, offers little protection against infection.

"At present, there is no direct evidence on the effectiveness of universal masking of healthy people in the community to prevent infection with respiratory viruses, including COVID-19," according to WHO's "Advice on the Use of Masks in the Context of COVID-19," published in June 2020, and "there are potential benefits and harms to consider" in December 2020.

Tom Jefferson and Carl Heneghan of the Centre for Evidence-Based Medicine at the University of Oxford evaluated the scientific literature on July 23, 2020, and commented, "Despite two decades of pandemic preparation, it appears that the value of wearing masks is still debatable.

In the United States, thirty-eight states have mandated mask use since the summer of 2020, and most others have mandated mask use in their major cities.

Data from Gallup, YouGov, the Covid-19 consortium, the CDC, and others indicate that about 80 percent or more of Americans have been wearing masks since the late summer 2020, which is at or above the level of most Western European countries and close to that of Asia.

If only those who reported wearing the masks "exactly as instructed" were considered, this did not influence the results; there was no difference between those wearing masks and those who did not.

For the eleven respiratory viruses, with the exception of SARS2, there was no significant difference between mask wearers and non-mask wearers.

"Now that we have adequately thorough scientific studies we can depend on, the evidence reveals that wearing masks in the community does not appreciably reduce the risks of illness," Heneghan and Jefferson stated emphatically. To further cement the case, University of Louisville researchers published a detailed analysis of the effectiveness of masks and mask regulations in the United States in May 2021, using CDC data spanning multiple seasons during the 2020 pandemic.

Their conclusion was, "Our main finding is that mask requirement and use are not associated with less spread of SARS-CoV-2 in U.S. states." They found that "80% of U.S. states mandated masks during the COVID-19 pandemic. These mandates led to greater mask compliance, but did not predict lower growth rates when community spread was low or high." The Louisville researchers' conclusion is clear.

In summary, mask mandates and [mask] use were ineffective predictors of COVID-19 spread in the United States. Our findings do not support the hypothesis that SARS-CoV-2 transmission rates decrease with increasing mask use in the public." Perhaps the clearest indication of the deeply damaged psyche of many Americans is their refusal to accept that masks are not necessary after vaccinations.

Antibody tests yield significant false-positive and false-negative results - would that also negate all statistical significance in this age group alone? And if less than half the villagers in villages where masks are worn are actually wearing them, would that logically justify a significant drop in symptomatic cases, when we know that masks do not even protect the mask wearers themselves? There is no doubt that the public is desperate for at least one study, direct evidence, after believing for eighteen months that masks work despite all evidence to the contrary.

No one seems to mind that even in nations where masks are not widely used, such as Sweden, influenza has disappeared Ironically, Dr. Fauci was accurately right back in March 2020 when he said, "There is no reason to walk around with a mask." He explained some of the scientific findings in his own emails, now revealed.

The conclusion: widespread use of masks does not protect mask wearers and does not effectively prevent SARS2 contamination.

Governor DeSantis has opted for a targeted protection strategy and has opposed calls for mandatory mask wearing and extended lockdowns measures.
On September 1, he stated, "We will never do any of these lockdowns again," ending the closure of businesses, rejecting mobility restrictions and removing the mask mandates.

Made in the USA
Middletown, DE
24 October 2022

13436502R00051